A Shifting Society

by Joshua Nissenbaum
illustrated by Ron Mahoney

Editorial Offices: Glenview, Illinois • Parsippany, New Jersey • New York, New York
Sales Offices: Needham, Massachusetts • Duluth, Georgia • Glenview, Illinois
Coppell, Texas • Ontario, California • Mesa, Arizona

Every effort has been made to secure permission and provide appropriate credit for photographic material. The publisher deeply regrets any omission and pledges to correct errors called to its attention in subsequent editions.

Unless otherwise acknowledged, all photographs are the property of Scott Foresman, a division of Pearson Education.

Photo locators denoted as follows: Top (T), Center (C), Bottom (B), Left (L), Right (R), Background (Bkgd)

Opener: Ron Mahoney; 1 Hunter Museum of American Art; 3 Library of Congress; 4 North Wind Picture Archives; 5 North Wind Picture Archives; 6 Ohio Historical Society; 7 Ron Mahoney; 8 Art Resource, NY; 13 Ron Mahoney; 14 Ron Mahoney; 15 Corbis; 17 Ron Mahoney; 19 Deleware Art Museum, Wilmington, USA/Bridgeman Art; 21 Library of Congress; 22 Corbis

ISBN: 0-328-13491-0

Copyright © Pearson Education, Inc.

All Rights Reserved. Printed in the United States of America. This publication is protected by Copyright, and permission should be obtained from the publisher prior to any prohibited reproduction, storage in a retrieval system, or transmission in any form by any means, electronic, mechanical, photocopying, recording, or likewise. For information regarding permission(s), write to: Permissions Department, Scott Foresman, 1900 East Lake Avenue, Glenview, Illinois 60025.

5 6 7 8 9 10 V0G1 14 13 12 11 10 09 08 07

A New Home

At the start of the 1800s, the United States was a very young country. Independence had been won from the British only seventeen years earlier, and the country was growing. Every year new people arrived from foreign countries, bringing new languages, new cultures, and new ideas to the United States.

New Americans have not all been treated equally or fairly, however. In the early 1800s, some people discriminated against others based on skin color or where they were from. Some people did not believe in treating people of differing ethnicities equally or fairly.

New immigrants arrived and people explored the country. People had to decide how to treat immigrants, enslaved people, and the Native Americans living on the newly explored lands.

American society has always valued personal freedom and equality, although in the 1800s it was often a struggle to achieve them. This period of time and the changes that occurred helped to shape the country.

Immigrants coming to the new land

3

Europeans sailing to America

The United States Expands

Even before the late 1800s, the United States had begun to grow and change. Between 1780 and 1820, the number of states in the country increased from thirteen to twenty-three. Between 1790 and 1820, the number of people living in the country nearly tripled.

The economy of the United States grew as factories were built in the North and tobacco and cotton production increased in the South. People built railroads, roads, and canals to transport people and goods.

Farming tobacco and cotton required **manual** labor, and these industries relied heavily on enslaved people to pick the crops. Enslaved people spent their whole lives on plantations working the land with their hands. Immigrant workers helped fill the factories of the North. The immigrants may have been free, but they worked in very tough conditions for very little pay.

Many new immigrants moved west in search of better options. There they became farmers and trappers. In order for the new settlements to survive, everyone had to help out. This led many people in western territories to appreciate one another. But those living in the North and South still had very different views on personal freedom and equality.

Around the world, slavery was beginning to be seen as morally wrong. In 1807 the English declared the slave trade illegal, though it would be many years before the British Parliament officially ended the practice of slavery.

However, Southern plantation owners in the United States relied heavily on the labor of enslaved people. Between 1820 and 1860, cotton production increased seventeen times and the enslaved population increased two-and-a-half times. By 1860 there were almost four million enslaved people living in the South.

Enslaved people picking cotton

Harriet Beecher Stowe

Enslaved people were the property of their owners. Their whole lives were spent working, and they were sold or traded as their owners saw fit. Owners saw enslaved people as a valuable source of labor.

By the mid-1800s slavery was a central issue in the politics of the United States. People who wanted to end slavery were called abolitionists. Abolitionists wanted slavery declared illegal everywhere.

In 1852 Harriet Beecher Stowe wrote a book called *Uncle Tom's Cabin*. It told the story of an enslaved man and the horrible experiences of his life. This book sold more than 1,500,000 copies around the world.

Uncle Tom's Cabin made it easier to understand why it was so important to end slavery—so that people would not be treated poorly or unfairly. It gave abolitionists a personal story to help them in their fight against slavery.

Other authors also began to write about freedom. Many writings challenged people to resist unjust laws instead of just accepting them.

These writers helped make people aware of the issues that abolitionists fought for. The incredible success of *Uncle Tom's Cabin* showed that many people wanted to learn about slavery and put an end to it.

A family reading *Uncle Tom's Cabin* together

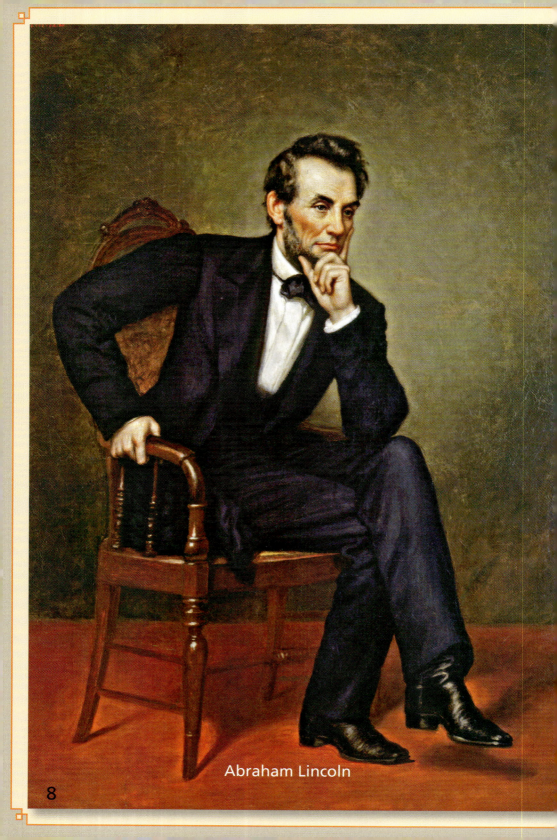
Abraham Lincoln

The Civil War: 1861-1865

In 1860 Abraham Lincoln was elected President of a country that was deeply divided. The South resented his presidency and was worried that he would try to end slavery. Seven Southern states decided to break away and form their own country between December 1860 and February 1861. Four more states joined in April 1861.

Alabama, Florida, Georgia, Louisiana, Mississippi, South Carolina, Texas, Virginia, Arkansas, North Carolina, and Tennessee formed a group called the Confederate States of America. They elected their own president. They even made their own constitution, which allowed slavery to continue. This secession, or withdrawal, was illegal, and it led to the Civil War.

The South felt strongly that they would win the Civil War. Cotton, produced in the South, was the largest exported good in the United States. In 1860 the South sold more than $120,000,000 worth of cotton to the world. The Southerners felt that the English and French would help them win the war because they wanted Southern cotton.

The South may have had a strong cotton economy, but the North had more and better resources. The North, or the Union, was larger and had more people. There were more factories to make goods for the Union army. There were many more miles of railroad to transport the goods.

The Civil War officially began on April 12, 1861. Both sides thought it would be over in months, but the war took four years. Some of the leaders had military experience, but most of the men were untrained as soldiers at the start.

The North vs. The South

	North (Union)	South (Confederacy)
Number of States	23	11
Population	22,000,000	5,100,000 whites 3,900,000 enslaved people
Economy	100,000 factories	20,000 factories
Railroad	20,000 miles	9,000 miles
Available Money	$50,000,000	$20,000,000

Lincoln issued the final version of the Emancipation Proclamation on January 1, 1863. This freed all enslaved people living in areas under Confederate control. The war was now about both reunification and ending slavery.

The Emancipation Proclamation also allowed ex-slaves to join the Union army. During the Civil War, 185,000 African American soldiers fought for the Union army.

From July 1, 1863, to July 3, 1863, the armies of the North and South fought the Battle of Gettysburg. This was a major win for the Union army and a turning point. On April 9, 1865, the leader of the Confederate army, General Robert E. Lee, surrendered to the leader of the Union army, General Ulysses S. Grant.

The end of the Civil War was a major event in the history of the United States. The federal government had successfully preserved the Union and ended slavery. But this war was the bloodiest war fought in American history. More than 600,000 American soldiers had died, and huge areas of the country were destroyed.

The chart below describes the three amendments that were added to the Constitution in order to protect the rights of the formerly enslaved people. They needed these amendments because even after the Civil War, many people treated formerly enslaved people as second-class citizens.

The Thirteenth, Fourteenth, and Fifteenth Amendments were adopted to protect the rights of the formerly enslaved people. Sadly, the government of the United States could wage a war and officially end slavery, but it could not force each person in the United States to treat others with respect.

The Reconstruction Era followed the Civil War. During this time, people rebuilt cities and farms, and Southerners returned to their homes.

Amendments to the Constitution

The Thirteenth Amendment outlawed slavery in the United States and any area under United States control. Three-fourths of the states passed it on December 6, 1865.

The Fourteenth Amendment granted citizenship to all people born in the United States. Newly freed people of the South were also made citizens with full rights. Passed by three-fourths of the states on July 9, 1868.

The Fifteenth Amendment granted all male citizens the right to vote. Passed by three-fourths of the states on February 3, 1870.

The newly freed people had a tough time during Reconstruction. Much of the South did not recognize their freedom, and their former masters made it very difficult for them to find new work.

Some formerly enslaved people stayed with their old masters as paid employees, while others left. Many freed people looked for family members that they had not seen in years.

After two hundred years of slavery in the United States, Americans had to change the way they thought about African Americans before African Americans could be treated as equals. Changing society's beliefs about African Americans took time.

Freed African Americans

Westward Expansion

During the late 1800s many immigrants entered the United States from Europe and Asia. From 1850 to 1900, approximately 16,500,000 immigrants came into the country. The majority arrived during the period from 1880 to 1900. These people came to the United States because it offered them more opportunities than their home countries did.

In 1862 the Homestead Act became law. This gave every American citizen the chance to own a farm. The Homestead Act stated that in certain areas of the United States, people could claim up to 160 acres of land. After five years these people could own the land as long as they built a home on the land and farmed part of it.

The Homestead Act encouraged settlement and development of the West. Immigrants from all over Europe came to the United States and immediately claimed their own land.

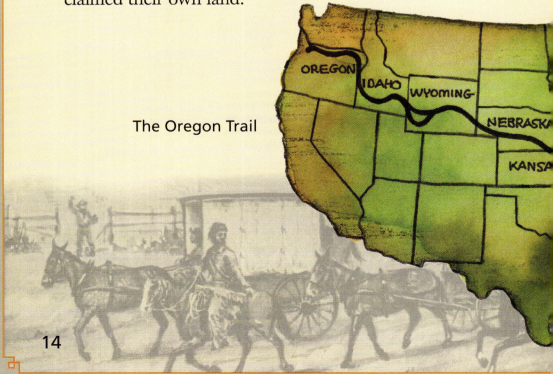

The Oregon Trail

Immigrants moved west and set up their own farms. They traveled on trails that had been created years earlier by explorers. One of the most famous trails was the Oregon Trail.

In 1812 Robert Stuart became the first person to use the route that became known as the Oregon Trail. He traveled on a horse and carried his supplies with him. His trail improved over the track that Lewis and Clark had mapped out a few years before. The trail stretched approximately two thousand miles and went through Missouri, Kansas, Nebraska, Wyoming, Idaho, and Oregon.

In 1836 Marcus Whitman and his wife Narcissa almost completed the entire Oregon Trail in a wheeled wagon. The Whitmans sparked more westward advancement. Once settlers realized that they could travel by wagon, they were able to take all the supplies that they needed to set up permanent homes in the West.

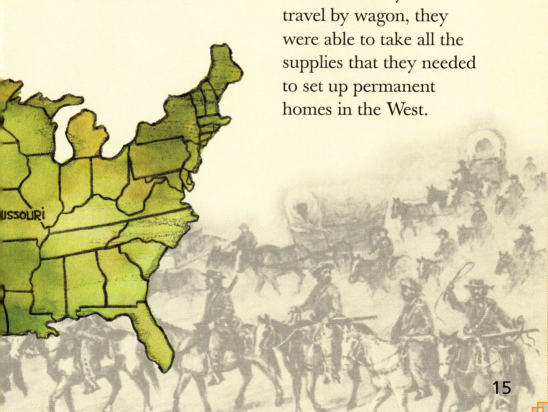

In 1843 a wagon train of one thousand people set out from Independence, Missouri, bound for Oregon. Crossing the Rocky Mountains was a challenge to their **endurance,** but the group managed to cross through a pass known as the South Pass. This was the only place between Missouri and Oregon gentle enough for wagon travel. This journey became known as the "Great Migration."

By 1861 roughly 350,000 immigrants had traveled west on the Oregon Trail. Even though the settlers traveled in groups and followed trails, their journey proved to be dangerous. Along the way they faced tough weather and the possibility that their wagons could break an axle or that their oxen could die. Sometimes—although rarely—the Native Americans who lived on the land through which the Oregon Trail passed attacked the wagon trains. But most of the people who died on the trail died from disease or accidents.

In 1890 the results of the national census showed that the frontier was closed. Throughout the West there were new communities made up of mixtures of people who had originally come from Sweden, Germany, Ireland, and many other European countries—as well as Central America, Asia, and Africa.

A wagon train leaving the Rocky Mountains heading for the Oregon plains

Native Americans

The government may have given enslaved people freedom, but it took away freedom from Native Americans. Nations of Native Americans had lived in every part of the United States for thousands of years. They had developed complex cultures and languages. However, their way of life differed from white Americans. The government did not value the Native American way of life and did not provide Native Americans with any rights.

As immigrants came to the United States and settled in "new" areas, they took land away from Native Americans. The government forced Native Americans off their land and paid very small sums of money for it.

Around 1812, a chief of the Shawnee nation named Tecumseh tried to unite Native Americans. He hoped to protect all Native American land from the Europeans. He traveled from the Great Lakes to the Gulf of Mexico and spoke with the different Native American groups.

Then the Indian Removal Act of 1830 allowed the United States government to force Native Americans from their land to "Indian Territory." The land that is now Oklahoma marked an area set up by the United States government for Native Americans.

Tecumseh and the settlers

The Homestead Act of 1862 is a good example of how the United States government placed the rights of settlers before the rights of Native Americans. The Homestead Act allowed settlers to claim ownership over land that had been part of the "Indian Territory." Native Americans had lived on this land for thousands of years, yet it was given away to the European settlers when they settled the West.

In addition to taking the land of the Native Americans, the government also tried to end their culture. In 1883 the Indian Religious Crimes Code punished Native Americans who continued to practice their religion. Punishments included being sent to jail or having the government withhold financial support.

The government passed this law to try to make the Native Americans live like the rest of American society. The government helped to set up **boarding schools** throughout the country to teach Native American children how to fit into American society. While at boarding school, the children lived together in a building called a **dormitory.** The teachers at these schools allowed the children to speak only English and did not teach them about their Native American cultures.

By the late 1800s the majority of Native Americans lived on **reservations** or in boarding schools. Life proved to be difficult for them. Shortages of both food and good farming land made it impossible for Native Americans to live as they had traditionally.

In 1926 the United States government wrote a report that studied the conditions on Native American reservations. This report criticized the reservation system and stated that the United States government's effort to force Native Americans to adopt the American way of life had been a total failure.

Native American schoolhouse

21

American Life in the 1800s

By 1899 the United States was a very different country from what it had been in 1800. Throughout the century more than nineteen million immigrants entered the country. They came from Europe, Asia, Canada, Latin America, and Africa. These immigrants greatly influenced the development of the United States.

Immigrants in the 1800s

At the start of the 1800s the immigrants had worked mainly agricultural jobs. As the cities grew, many went there to work in the factories. The little chance of advancement for these immigrants made life difficult for them.

Events before and after the Civil War caused many people to think more about personal freedom and equality.

Following the Civil War even more immigrants entered the country. The government welcomed these people and encouraged them to settle in the West. Wagon trains crossed the country and by 1890 the government declared that the settlers had settled so many places that there no longer were frontier areas.

During the 1800s America absorbed millions of immigrants and became a true "melting pot." By the end of the 1800s America had grown to fill its borders and had learned the importance of equality and personal freedom.

Glossary

boarding schools *n.* schools with buildings where pupils live during a school term.

dormitory *n.* a building with many rooms in which people sleep.

endurance *n.* power to last and to withstand hard wear.

manual *adj.* done with the hands.

reservations *n.* lands set aside by the government for a special purpose.

society *n.* the people of any particular time or place.